BULLETPROOF

BUSINESS PROTECTION STRATEGIES FROM A WAR ZONE

STEPHEN D. LENTZ, ESQ.

HIGH BRIDGE BOOKS
HOUSTON

Bulletproof
by Stephen D. Lentz

Printed in the United States of America
ISBN (Paperback): 978-1-946615-64-0

High Bridge Books titles may be purchased in bulk for educational, business, fundraising, or sales promotional use. For information, please contact High Bridge Books via www.HighBridgeBooks.com/contact.

Published in Houston, Texas by High Bridge Books

CONTENTS

INTRODUCTION

When you are taking flak, you know you are over the target!

My head of security and director of news, Salam Eid, informed me, "We need to go and meet General Lahad before we go to the station. He is the General for the South Lebanese Army."

I was in South Lebanon. I was the newly appointed president of Middle East Television, the largest superstation[1] in the Middle East. It was my first week on the job, and the operations for our station was in a war zone!

"You are here in South Lebanon as his guest. You have no papers."

I had left my passport at the checkpoint on the Israel border and had no visa … because we were in a war zone!

"Our station is located on his property. It is customary for our leaders to pay him respect when they are in town," Salam continued.

OK, I can do that, I thought to myself. I was used to meeting company heads and advertising heads as the former Senior Vice President of Advertising Sales for the Family Channel.[2] How hard could this be?

"I will do the translating. He knows me and trusts me. He won't be shaking your hand with his right hand. He is just recovering from an assassination attempt,"[3] Salam explained.

He definitely had my interest!

"He customarily takes naps in the afternoon. The Hezbollah [4]conduct their ground attacks and maneuvers at night. He is usually up all night. Recently, after one of his afternoon naps, he came down to greet his beautiful, young French wife. She had just finished working out with her trainer. It turned out the trainer was Hezbollah. She had a pistol concealed in her rolled-up towel. When General Lahad came to greet his wife, the trainer pulled out the gun and shot him three times at point-blank range. He reached up with his right arm to protect himself and the bullet went through his arm and traveled up and out of his elbow but protected his life."

Now Salam really had my attention!

General Antoine Lahad[5]

We were understandably frisked at the door to his house by a giant, dark swarthy and fully armed security guard. We were guided into a sunroom overlooking the Lebanon Mountains. The general was a short man with intense but kind eyes and the customary shadowy beard. His arm was in a sling and he extended his left hand. We sat down to wonderful Turkish coffee. He called for additional "hospitality." I have gone to many friend's homes and enjoyed a nice fruit tray or cheese tray or some nice hors d'oeuvres. I was hungry from all the stress and was looking forward to some good comfort food. Much to my surprise, the server brought us a huge bowl filled with a variety of not fruit and cheese, but cigarettes!

As we sat down to talk, the windows were vibrating from the concussion of shelling happening close by in the mountains. Needless to say, I was way out of my comfort zone! Anticipating the first question from the general to be complicated on so many fronts about world events, security issues in the zone regarding our operations, and the current shelling and fighting, I waited.

"Tell me about Monica Lewinsky" was the general's first question! And so began my education about doing business in a war zone!

When we attempt to accomplish anything important … anything that matters … we need to realize that we have just stepped onto a battlefield … into a war zone!

This book is dedicated to every business professional, pastor, and leader who is attempting to accomplish something important in his or her professional career or calling.

When we attempt to accomplish anything important ... anything that matters ... we need to realize that we have just stepped onto a battlefield ... into a war zone! I know you will be able to identify with the feeling of "being shot at," or the feelings of "danger" and being pursued by some kind of enemy, real or imagined.

I hope some of the lessons I learned doing business in an actual war zone will give you comfort, direction, and courage to continue to take ground and not give up and not leave the field when the shooting starts.

As a leader once said: "When you are taking flak, you know you are over the target"!

---

[1] A "super-station" is a local television station that sends its local signal up to a satellite and then beams it across a large area, changing the station from a local station to a "super-station." Middle East Television was the largest super-station in the middle east, covering all of Israel and every Arab country.

---

[2] I was the senior official over our offices in New York, Chicago, Detroit, Los Angeles, London, and Hong Kong. My sales force generated over $100,000,000 annually, which lead to the valuation and sale of the Family Channel to Rupert Murdock in 1997 for approximately $1.9 billion.

[3] In 1988, Souha Bechara, a 21-year-old woman, tried to assassinate Lahad. She had been raised in the Eastern Orthodox Church and had become a member of the Communist party. She was tasked with assassinating Lahad. Bechara disguised herself as an aerobics instructor to visit with Lahad's family. On November 17, 1988, while she was having tea with Lahad's wife, Bechara shot the general twice in the chest. She was detained by his security team. Lahad spent eight weeks in the hospital and suffered health complications leaving his left arm paralyzed. Upon his return to service, he pardoned and released Souha Bechara after the Lebanese and French government pleaded with him to do so, and after she spent ten years in Khiam prison and suffered six years of solitary confinement in a tiny cell.

[4] **Hezbollah** was founded in the early 1980s as part of an Iranian effort to aggregate a variety of militant Lebanese Shia groups into a unified organization. **Hezbollah** acts as a proxy for Iran in the ongoing Iran–Israel proxy conflict. They had been waging war in South Lebanon since 1985.

---

[5] While commanding the SLA, General Lahad formed three regiments mainly from Druze, Shia and Christians who fought together to take back control of Lebanese territory from all the Palestinian factions who controlled much of southern Lebanon. During his service, he never cut contact with the capital, and all leaders from all political factions and religions kept visiting him asking him for help on several matters. He reinstated the salaries of the Lebanese army soldiers in the south, which had previously been cut off. He built three major hospitals in Hasbaya, Marjyoun and Nabatieh and rejuvenated the economy of southern Lebanon, which was historically left to its own devices by all Lebanese central governments.

1

LEADERSHIP IS ALWAYS THE PROBLEM … LEADERSHIP IS ALWAYS THE ANSWER!

I know the question from General Lahad seems funny and ridiculously out of place for the setting, but it underscored for me an essential principle. Leaders do not act in a vacuum. People are watching. People are taking their cues from the actions and language of their leaders. In the case of heads of organizations or churches or movements or countries, the actions of leaders can be a tremendous positive and productive force or release chaos and uncertainty.

In the case of President Clinton's dalliances with Ms. Lewinsky, I am sure he was not thinking that his actions in his office at the

White House would have any foreign policy implications or would affect things on a worldwide scale. However, for General Lahad, trying to anticipate the support (or lack thereof) of world powers like the United States, the President's actions carried far-reaching implications.

"Would your President start a war to try to divert attention from his personal problems," General Lahad asked. "Or would he *not engage* in an important supportive conflict out of fear that he would be blamed for starting an action to divert attention from his personal problems?"

Tell Me About Monica Lewinsky!

This sentiment was not an isolated incident for me while trying to work in the war zone. Part of my responsibility was to establish a protocol to evacuate my personnel at the station in South Lebanon across the Israeli border if our positions were overrun by the Hezbollah.[1] On one occasion, I met with the generals for the Northern Command for the Israel Defense Forces (IDF). Salam drove me across the border from South Lebanon at night. We drove for a long time in the mountains and forest. As a typical American, I am not used to traveling anywhere where there is no ambient light of some kind. There was no ambient light happening in Northern Israel in the forest. It was so very dark and foreboding.

I needed to meet with the generals of the Northern Command to establish the essential evacuation plan for our people. Finally, after driving for what seemed like an eternity in the pitch dark, we reached a clearing with an old stone farmhouse. It had a stone well in the rear of the building, and the grounds included another stone outbuilding that could have served as a barn. Upon entering the "barn," we went underground! I found myself in a tavern, with huge wine kegs lining the stone walls. White tablecloths and candles were on our tables. The ceilings were very low ... I felt like I had just entered a John Grisham novel!

The highlight of the evening was when the generals arrived with their attaches. Dashing military men and women in their fatigues, coming right off maneuvers. Their caps were inserted in their epilates on their shoulders. I learned another important series of lessons about leadership. First of all, they spoke impeccable English. I felt so honored as I heard them recite observation after observation about the respect they had for our country. Their understanding and command of US history and civics made me feel so respected. They knew more about the history of our presidents than I did. From that night on, I promised myself that I would never meet with another business associate or pastor or leader without thoroughly researching their country. I promise you that understanding who your audience is and what they believe will be time well spent!

Waiting for the "important" issues of the night to unfold, one of the generals turned to me. "Steve, I have an important question to ask you."

I didn't know if I was going to be up to the moment. Hearing them so sincerely and eloquently speak about my country and its history, I began to squirm in my seat.

"Tell me about Monica Lewinsky!" The generals recited the same concerns that General Lahad had communicated at his house in South Lebanon. "We are afraid he will start a war to get the heat off him. Alternately, we are afraid he will hold back in supporting us out of fear of being blamed for trying to deflect attention from his personal problems!"

Leaders' actions have a profound effect on so many people. If we are going to lead well, we must consider the far-reaching implications of our actions, for good or for bad!

I love the example we have from our Savior:

> Truly, truly, I tell you, no servant is greater than his master, nor is a messenger greater than the one who sent him.[2]

---

[1] Our positions were eventually overrun by the Hezbollah in 2000. Because of the protocols set in place, all of our personnel were able to evacuate, under machine gun fire, but with no loss of life!

[2] John 13:16 NIV.

2

REALIZE YOU *ARE* IN A WAR!

Probably one of the most exciting and meaningful assignments I have ever had in my professional life was being appointed as President of Middle East Television.[1] The assignment had so many different business elements, and I loved each component. My job included marketing and advertising, which I conducted in Tel Aviv. Politics was always in the background. As the only non-Jewish television station with a major presence in Israel, part of my responsibility was to maintain and secure our relationship with the government headquartered in Jerusalem. I regularly met with government officials in Jerusalem, including meeting personally with Prime Minister Netanyahu regarding the potential relocation of the station into Israel.

Meeting with Prime Minister Netanyahu at the Knesset in Israel with Michael Little, former President of Christian Broadcasting Network

I had the opportunity to use my legal background by employing and managing relationships with three different law firms in Israel. Each had its own particular assignment: I had a local Israeli attorney (my local Columbo) who would collect fees from overdue advertising accounts; I had a team of lawyers in Jerusalem who were orthodox Jews and former members of the Knesset, who could defend me from attacks and harassment from the religious forces in Israel who were unhappy that a non-Jewish television station had a presence in the country; and I had a crack team of Israeli fighter pilots who were also on the cutting edge of the communications law in Israel to fight with the courts to allow Middle East TV to advertise and program in Hebrew. In Israel, only Channel 1 and Channel 2 could advertise in Hebrew. My crack team and I went to the Supreme Court of Israel and successfully secured the right to broadcast and to advertise in Hebrew.

However, the most exciting part of the assignment was managing and conducting operations of an actual television station in a war zone in South Lebanon!

On my first day, I had to drive hours up to the northern border of Israel. I spent the night in a little town called Metula, a town in the Northern District of Israel. It is located between the biblical cities of Dan, Abel Bet Ma'akha, and Eyon, bordering Lebanon. Metula is the northernmost town in Israel with a population of under 2,000 people.

That first night, I stayed in a small, quaint local hotel that looked and felt more like a small lodge in preparation for my first trip across the border the next morning into South Lebanon and into a war zone. It was freezing cold in Metula that night. I remember contacting my wife back in the states. We thought becoming president of Middle East Television would be a great assignment! This would be interesting … working in the Holy Land. [2]But that night, realizing that part of the job was doing business in a war zone had Cathy and me praying in earnest in a way we had not experienced in our marriage up until that time.

The next morning, I woke up in Metula and was taken to the border by my head of operations who was residing in Israel and commuted back and forth into South Lebanon frequently. We met the Israeli Defense Forces (IDF) at the border. They examined me. They examined my entire luggage. And then they took my passport! I had no visa because I was entering a war zone. I could not take my passport because I was entering a war zone. No visa. No passport. I was going in as "the guest of General Lahad," the General of the South Lebanese Army (who I had yet to meet).

My wonderful wife, Cathy, and me overlooking the Port of Jaffa and the Mediterranean[3]

After completing our inspection by the IDF, we walked across two checks points with a no-man's land between the two checkpoints. Maybe you have seen pictures of something like this from scenes from the Berlin Wall and the no-man's land from the Cold War era. On this day, I walked through two gates. One gate would lift up and I would walk out of Israel. After a football-field-length walk, I would approach the second gate, which lifted upon inspection, and I stepped into South Lebanon. No papers. No visa.

I was met by my head of news who was also my head of security. His name is Salam Eid. Salam was a strong, quiet, sharp-eyed Lebanese who would later become one of my closest friends. Salam introduced himself very respectfully and then handed me a flak jacket! After I struggled to put on my first flak jacket, he instructed me to put my luggage in the back of the car.

This was my first day in the war zone. I am on the far left with my newly acquired "flak jacket." Salam, my trusted friend and guard, is in the middle ... the only one not wearing body armor!

Well ... our "car" was a Range Rover that my station had acquired second hand from the French Embassy. It was an armor car with 2,000 pounds of lead and bulletproof windows that already had been shot at and boasted the bullet holes to prove it! The back door was so heavy I couldn't open it to put my luggage away. I finally got in the car and there was an AK-47 between Salam and me. Nervously, I put my seat belt on.

Salam popped the seat belt. "We don't wear seat belts here in case we are attacked. Now … would you like to go see the broadcast tower?" Salam said.

I'm thinking, *I don't know where the tower is, and I don't know where I am! I'm not sure I'm really happy about this assignment after all!* I was the president of Middle East Television. I was technically managing all the operations. So I bravely (and naively) said: "Sure, I guess."

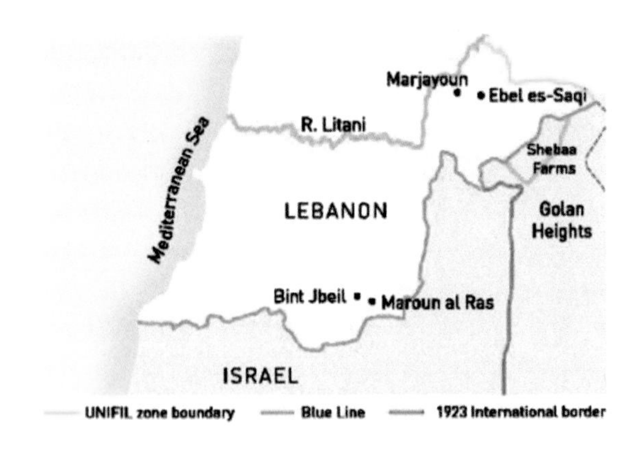

The tower was in Maroun al-Ras. The station was in Marjayoun.

We had a three-car convoy. It turned out that the tower was on the top of Maroun El Ras, which was on a mountain in South Lebanon! For several hours, we weaved through the countryside, through Hezbollah villages to get to our tower. We were driving in this three-car caravan. I was in an armored car with an armed guard and we kept changing the order of the cars.

I asked Salam, "Why do we keep changing the order of the cars?"

He said, "I don't want anyone to know which car you are in. I don't want them to bomb us or attack us and take you prisoner."

It was January, it was cold, and my teeth were chattering, but I don't think it was from the cold! I am convinced it was because I was absolutely terrified. I am not from a military background. I have never had the privilege of serving in the armed forces.[4] To my recollection, I have only been in two real "fights" in my whole life, and that was in high school. This was definitely not my normal experience.

As we were driving through the countryside, through rubble that once held family dwellings, with our four-wheel drive bouncing down the unpaved rocky roads, I was struck by the devastation and disorder. I asked Salam about the houses that were reduced to rubble. Salam explained that the Israelis would demolish any house used as a staging point for an attack or that housed snipers. Driving. Teeth still chattering. Finally, we got to a mountain clearing and all these men, fully armed with AK-47 rifles, guns, ammo belts, knives, and grenades, appeared out of the bushes and surrounded our car!

"Are they our guys or theirs," I breathlessly whispered.

"Our guys," Salam said. "They are local militia, Shiite guards that we employ to guard our tower."

We got out of the car to approach the "tower," and it looked to me like Fort Apache! Machine gun turrets were located strategically at every corner and snaked; barbed wire fencing protected the one entrance into the complex. When we finally got into the tower complex, we were surrounded by about 15 guards, and Salam explained to me that these are some of *my* "employees"! When everyone was counted, I had 70 employees at Middle East Television, and 32 were armed Shiite guards.[5]

Salam went on to explain that the guards wanted to have a picture with the new president.

Some of my "employees" ... fully armed!

I definitely looked like a deer caught in the headlights, with a frozen, concerned, fake smile. Out of the corner of my eye, I saw Salam walking a guy out of the group and off the premises at gunpoint! After we took the picture, finished our tour of the facility, and got back into the car, I asked Salam what was happening behind the scenes. He told me that the guy wanted a "private meeting" with the president. Salam explained that no one gets a private meeting with the president, but the guy was so insistent that Salam felt he had a dangerous motive. So he told him he would have to disarm to have a private meeting. After Salam disarmed the man, he terminated his employment and walked him off the site.

"If we don't handle these types of situations at the time, we could have a real problem with the rest of the men. They were watching."

We left the station. I was a wreck inside, trying to get my emotions in check, put on a brave face, and act like an executive, but inside I thought, *I just want to go back to Virginia to my wife and family*!

Salam looked at me and casually asked, "Would you like to go see the station now?"

I thought, *Well, I* am *the president of Middle East Television. I guess I should go to the station.* So I said, "Sure."

I have gone to lengths to describe this moment to underscore one vital fact of my tenure at Middle East Television. When I took the position of president and crossed over into South Lebanon, everything changed. I had stepped into a war zone.

The first lesson that I learned is that I had to realize that I was in a war zone to properly function!

I am informed by my faith. I believe the Bible is the best leadership book ever written. It is a guide, a light, and a pathway to life. Jesus told us that this world is a war zone!

> In the world you will have trials, tribulations, vexation of soul and frustration. But be of good cheer, I have overcome the world![6]

You can't read the Apostle Paul's resume and conclude anything less than this world will serve up difficulties that amount to a war on our souls if we commit to accomplishing anything of importance for our family, our businesses, our churches, or our communities. Paul's most important credentials were not his accomplishments but in the sufferings that he endured to invest in others:

> Whatever anyone else boasts … I also dare to boast about … Are they servants of Christ? (I am out

> of my mind to talk like this.) I am more. I have worked much harder, been in prison more frequently, been flogged more severely, and been exposed to death again and again. Five times I received from the Jews the forty lashes minus one. Three times I was beaten with rods, once I was pelted with stones, three times I was shipwrecked. I spent a night and a day in the open sea. I have been constantly on the move. I have been in danger from rivers, in danger from bandits, in danger from my fellow Jews, in danger from Gentiles; in danger in the city, in danger in the country, in danger at sea; and in danger from false believers. I have labored and toiled and often gone without sleep; I have known hunger and thirst and have often gone without food; I have been cold and naked.[7]

In my experience, we need to take our assignments much more soberly. If we are trying to build a life for our family; if we are trying to build a business that will honor God and build a legacy for the future of others; if we are trying to build a church and to invest in the lives of others to see them live their highest and best life for Jesus and for eternity; if we are trying to influence our town, our culture, our society, or our world; then we *are* in a war! We have stepped into a war zone. See it for what it is and don't be surprised if someone ends up shooting at you!

---

[1] Thanks to M. G. Pat Robertson, Founder and Chairman, and the Board of Directors for Christian Broadcasting Network for the privilege of serving as president of Middle East Television.

[2] I would end up living in and out of Israel for almost two years. Cathy joined me many times.

[3] Old Jaffa Port (also known as Namal Yafo) was the ancient port of the city of Jaffa, out of which modern-day Tel Aviv has grown. The Old Jaffa Port is reputed to be one of the oldest ports in the world, notably being the port from which Jonah set off in the famous biblical story of Jonah and the Whale.

---

[4] My right knee basketball injury kept me out of the draft in the Vietnam War. I later had my knee replaced but regret not having had the privilege of serving in the Armed Forces.

[5] Having employees who are fully armed makes personnel matters a little touchy. We had to disarm our guards before we could terminate them!

[6] John 16:33.

[7] 2 Corinthians 11:23-27 (NIV).

3

NO ONE GOES TO WAR ALONE!

If life and great accomplishments can be compared to warfare, then one of the obvious lessons that I learned as president of Middle East Television is that no one goes to war alone! We need a team around us. My team of 72 employees included guards and Intel experts, news experts, operations experts, political and military contacts, and "friends" at multiple levels that helped to ensure our success, our safety, and our ultimate security. At Middle East Television, I had walked into a foreign environment. I was sure glad that I was surrounded by people who knew what they were doing!

King Solomon in the Bible was one of the richest and most successful kings of Israel, and a war-tested king. His wealth was legendary. The Bible says He built a temple and overlaid it with gold. All of King Solomon's goblets were gold, and, "Nothing was made of silver because silver was considered of little value in Solomon's days" (1 Kings 10:21).

King Solomon was a millionaire, and his kingdom extended from the Euphrates River to the border of Egypt. He owned property in an area roughly the size of Vermont. That's a huge piece of land, and he was earning over $58,000,000 a year in gold. Solomon is probably someone we would listen to if he was on the speaking circuit today! He knew the power of "team" and warns us that no good thing happens to people who isolate themselves:

> A man who isolates himself seeks his own desire; He rages against all wise judgment.[1]

Solomon instructs us in another passage of scripture:

> Where no counsel is, the people fall: but in the multitude of counsellors there is safety.[2]

Lesson 2: No one goes to war alone! We need a team around us.

I depended on the team around me at Middle East Television. In fact, I trusted my life to Salam and my team. If we are truly in a war, our team can not only protect us … they can save us in times of trouble.

When I became one of the executives at the Family Channel, my first leader was Doug Greenlaw. He recruited me and I eventually took over his position as Senior Vice President of Advertising Sales for the Family Channel. Doug is a handsome and dashing guy. Everyone in the advertising community loves him. I enjoyed working for him immensely and was privileged to learn so much about leadership from him. I think one of the most significant talks we ever had was about the importance of a team.

Doug was a wounded war veteran. I didn't know much about his war record until our discussion in his office at 6th Ave. at 44th in New York City. He had a habit of rubbing his face at the end of each day. It was a noticeable habit. I asked him one day why he rubbed his face. The story that followed forever etched in my soul how much we need each other. How much we need a team around us. He said it was because much of his face had been surgically repaired after being wounded. I asked him how he got wounded. His narrative forever changed my life.

He explained that he was in charge of a platoon that would have to cut through a "triple canopy jungle" to hunt down the enemy. He would always instruct new recruits not to walk on the trails … because they were always booby-trapped. He explained that it was so hard to be cutting through the "triple canopy jungle" when the trail was in sight. Terrain that could be traveled in a few minutes on the path could take hours to slug through cutting through the jungle.

> One day, I just got tired. So I did what I taught everyone else not to do … I walked on the path. It was a mistake. I stepped on an IUD and it blew me to pieces.

Doug recounted how his team came around him. They didn't stand over him and lecture him on how stupid it was to walk on the path! They picked him up (in pieces) and got him to the nearest medic. The medic transported him to the nearest hospital. He stayed there for a very long time but today is a dashing, handsome, and successful executive, leader, and friend. [3]

TEAM. We are famous for standing over our wounded and lecturing them, rather than getting them to help!

Many of our leaders get wounded because they get fatigued. They are in the battle … they have been heroically slashing through the triple canopy jungle of people's needs, addictions, wounds, troubles, and life's "vexations." Sometimes they get tired. Sometimes fatigue makes them do something stupid and they get wounded. What is our response? Do we have a team around us to help "pick up the pieces" and get them to help?

---

[1] Proverbs 18:1 NKJ.

[2] Proverbs 11:14 KJ.

[3] Doug received a battlefield promotion to Company Commander, following a minor wound that healed in Country. As CO, he used to go out at night occasionally with a small team to patrol or set

ambushes to show the men he wouldn't ask them to do anything that he hadn't done or wouldn't do. His point man tripped a tripwire and the trap exploded, injuring four of them. His wounds were grave. A Catholic priest gave him the last rights at the mash unit, but, obviously, he survived. *"The fast-moving young docs did a fine job saving my life"* – Doug Greenlaw

4

DRESS FOR BATTLE, NOT FOR A DANCE!

I love the compelling description of the world of warfare we are in as translated in the Message Bible:

> A Fight to the Finish
> And that about wraps it up. God is strong, and he wants you strong. So take everything the Master has set out for you, well-made weapons of the best materials. And put them to use so you will be able to stand up to everything the Devil throws your way. This is no afternoon athletic contest that we'll walk away from and forget about in a couple of hours. This is for

> keeps, a life-or-death fight to the finish against the Devil and all his angels.[1]

God wants us to be strong. But we can't be strong unless we use all the weapons He has made for us. Use "everything" the Master has set out … well-made weapons of the best materials." Why … we are in a war!

C. H. Spurgeon put it this way:

> TO BE A CHRISTIAN is to be a warrior. The good soldier of Jesus Christ must not expect to find ease in this world: it is a battlefield. Neither must he reckon upon the friendship of the world; for that would be enmity against God. His occupation is war. As he puts on piece by piece of the panoply provided for him, he may wisely say to himself, "This warns me of danger; this prepares me for warfare; this prophecies opposition."[2]

I live in a military area of the country. Hampton Roads in Virginia is the home of the Atlantic Fleet, Oceana Air Base, Seal Team

Six, and Fort Eustis. Not far up the road in Williamsburg is Camp Perry, where many of our special ops assignments are staged. It isn't hard to make military analogies in my area.

Lesson 3: Don't go to war in our everyday world only half-equipped for the battle!

The last time I researched, the cost to equip one special forces soldier with the state-of-the-art equipment used to give him an advantage in war was about $1.0 million per year per soldier. Every piece of equipment has been specially designed to give him the advantage in battle. The equipment has been specially designed to protect him and also to give him the edge in the battle to overcome!

It would seem ridiculous for any elite soldier to take only part of the equipment and leave the rest behind. For a trained soldier to refuse to wear the helmet because it was too hot; or to refuse to wear the goggles because the color blue isn't his favorite color; or to refuse the Kevlar vest because it was too confining would be unthinkable! And yet how often do we go to war in our everyday world only half-equipped for the battle?

How many times throughout the history of the church has the church left important and vital equipment, "well-made weapons of the best materials," on the shelf and gone into battle only partially equipped?

In the passage below, the Apostle Paul is urging us to recognize that the stakes are high.

> This is no afternoon athletic contest that we'll walk away from and forget about in a couple of hours. This is for keeps, a life-or-death fight to the finish against the Devil and all his angels.[3]

---

[1] Ephesians 6: 10-12 (MSG).

[2] A Sermon (No. 2201). Delivered on Lord's-Day Morning, April 19th, 1891, by C. H. SPURGEON, At the Metropolitan Tabernacle, Newington.

[3] Ephesians 6:12 (MSG).

5

BE ALERT!

Let's talk about some of the equipment that I benefited from firsthand when doing business in a war zone.

First, Jesus admonishes us to "keep alert":

> Be on guard, so that your hearts will not be weighted down with dissipation and drunkenness and the worries of life, and that day will not come on you suddenly like a trap; for it will come upon all those who dwell on the face of all the earth. But *keep on the alert at all times,* praying that you may have strength to escape all these things that are about to take place, and to stand before the Son of Man.[1]

The first thing that caught my attention was his eyes. They never stopped looking and surveying the territory we traveled in. Salam Eid, my head of security, was different from me. He was different from my friends. Why? Because he knew he was operating in a war zone. He had been wounded by a roadside bomb a year before I met him. *He was alert.* His eyes never rested. And he never smiled.[2] When I traveled with Salam, I knew we would not be taken by surprise. As we drove through the countryside to examine our tower or to go to the station, he was vigilant. His eyes ... they never stopped looking for anything out of place; anything unusual; anything that could present a danger to me.

Lesson 4: It is dangerous to forget that we are in a war and forget that we need to keep a vigilant watch over our surroundings!

I have met many parents, executives, and church leaders who have been lulled into a casual attitude toward raising, caring, nurturing, and building their families, businesses, and churches. It is dangerous to forget that we are in a war and need to keep a vigilant watch over our surroundings! The agenda of our archenemy, the devil, is clear. Jesus identifies him as a thief:

> The thief comes only to steal and kill and destroy;[3]

But I love what the wonderful and redemptive agenda of Jesus is in our lives:

> I have come that they may have life, and have it to the full.[4]

Is there anything "out of place" in our family? Out of place in our business? Out of place in our churches? Has someone or something crept into our world that can disrupt and destroy the work we are doing? These are sober times, and only vigilant attention can help us overcome and win the battles we are facing.

Lesson 5: "Staying alert" also speaks to me about not letting your guard down.

"Staying alert" also speaks to me about not letting your guard down. I learned this lesson while doing business in China for the Family Channel. For a time, I had the privilege of representing The Family Channel in its business development into mainland China.[5] It was an emerging cable television market. China had the largest potential television population in the world! It was well worth trying to make contact with the bureaucrats inside China to see if we could be part of the emerging cable landscape.

I developed a contact in Hong Kong named Danny Hoy, an exciting 30-year-old who was an entrepreneur on steroids! I called him the Cecil B. DeMille of Hong Kong. He had a production company, a film company, a talent agency, and was serving as a liaison with the bureaucrats inside China to make introductions. Danny's family was very connected inside mainland China and had a family history reaching all the way back to freedom fighters under Chiang Kai-shek.[6]

We were close friends. He gave me a Chinese name and even had a personal and formal chop made for me to sign documents in Chinese.[7] We were so close that he even invited me to his family ancestral worship in mainland China. It was the first time the Hoy family had gathered to ancestral worship in 50 years. I was the only non-Hoy invited. I was the only non-Chinese in attendance. That is how close we were.

However, I learned an important lesson about not letting my guard down in my relationship with Danny. Everywhere we went, he would introduce me as an important executive from America and a trusted friend. Then he would also add: "and he is Gweilo."[8] I finally asked what that reference meant. He said: "Foreign Devil"!

I said, "What? Do you mean that everywhere we have gone you have been introducing me as the devil?"

Danny politely answered, "Yes. Because you are not Chinese!"

He was right. I was not family. I was not Chinese. The minute I thought I was going to receive special treatment in my business relationships because of my friendship with Danny, I had naively put myself at a huge disadvantage!

It is important for us to never forget that we are foreigners. Be alert. Never let our guard down in this world that we live in.

Those of us who rely on the Holy Scriptures for advice and direction, understand that this world is just a staging area for eternity. We understand this world is not our home!

The Apostle Peter said it this way in the Scriptures:

> Dear friends, I urge you, as aliens and strangers in the world, to abstain from sinful desires, which war against your soul. Live such good lives among the pagans that, though they accuse you of doing wrong, they may see your good deeds and glorify God on the day he visits us.[9]

We are strangers in this world and have stepped on a battlefield for the souls of men, for the destiny of our families, and for the future kingdom of our Lord Jesus.

This is not our home! The Bible talks about the permanent home and eternal dwelling place of the Christian as our dwelling place in heaven:

> Jesus said, "Let not your heart be troubled; believe in God, believe also in Me. In My Father's house are many dwelling places; if it were not so, I would have told you; for I go to prepare a place for you. And if I go and prepare a place for you, I will come again, and receive you to Myself; that where I am, there you may be also."[10]

---

[1] Luke 21: 34-36 (NASB, emphasis added).

[2] In fact, it was years after he relocated to America that his daughters finally taught him to smile!

[3] John 10:10(a) (NIV).

---

[4] John 10:10(b) (NIV).

[5] Thanks to Tim Robertson, a good friend and former president and CEO of International Family Entertainment who trusted me with the assignment to explore business opportunities in China.

[6] Chiang Kai-shek was a soldier and statesman, the head of the Nationalist government in China from 1928 to 1949 and subsequently head of the Chinese Nationalist government in exile on Taiwan.

[7] A company chop is used to sign all legal documents. A personal chop is the name chop of the company's legal representative and is sometimes used as a signature for letters. This is not a stamp that mimics a physical signature — it simply has the carved-out letters of the representative's name.

[8] Gweilo or gwailou (Chinese: 鬼佬; Cantonese Yale: gwáilóu, pronounced [kʷɐ̌i lǒu] is a common Cantonese slang term and ethnic slur for Westerners. In its unmodified form, it refers to people of European descent and has a history of racially deprecatory and pejorative use.

[9] I Peter 2:11,12.

[10] John 14: 1-3.

6

"ENGAGE!"

Making a difference in this world, whether in your marriage, family, business, or church, is not for the faint of heart! If you want to make a difference … if you want to leave behind a legacy and build anything lasting and that has value … you will have to be present now … in the moment!

I think one of the most frustrating visuals from my time in South Lebanon was seeing the U. N. forces always on the perimeter. They were looking. They were monitoring. You could see their white jeeps and armored cars with the blue "U.N." distinctly emblazoned on their vehicles. The troops wore royal blue helmets to distinguish them from any other troops on the field. We knew they were there. Everyone knew they were there.

The locals gave this army a nickname—the "Un-Army." Why? Because they would never engage! They were there only to observe. They were insignificant. They were not there to make a difference and would have no lasting or important impact on anything happening in the zone.

Lesson 6: If you want to make a difference ... if you want to leave behind a legacy and build anything lasting and that has value ... you will have to be present now ... in the moment!

Too often, we approach life this way. We observe but don't really engage. We can't expect to make a difference in this world by sitting on the sidelines. It doesn't work in our marriages or our homes. It doesn't work in building a business. It doesn't work in building and sustaining our churches. God has meant for us to "engage" and to "participate." We were made to be "in the battle," not to be casual and unattached observers from the sidelines.

The armor of God listed in Ephesians chapter 6 only protects our front. Nothing is covering the warrior's backside! Why? Because I believe God has designed us to take ground and to move forward.

7

USE ALL THE EQUIPMENT! PART 1

"The Belt of Truth"

The "whole armor of God" listed in Ephesians 6 includes a reference to the "belt of truth." I don't know about you, but it seems like it is pretty difficult to wage war and run into the battle with your pants around your ankles!

To me, the belt of truth speaks about resisting the temptation to compromise. I don't believe we need to compromise our principles or our convictions to be leaders and successful in business. Our wonderful staff in South Lebanon were willing to risk their lives and their freedom for *truth*.

The news that came out of Middle East Television on a nightly basis was the most reliable news from the sector and was followed by leaders in Israel, Jordan, and many of the Arab countries as the "true story" of what was happening in the sector. For this, our staff paid the price of losing their freedom to travel out of the South Lebanon zone to see their families in Lebanon; they all had death sentences on them because they worked with Middle East Television (and were therefore seen as Israeli collaborators). Eventually, they all had to flee for their lives, under a hail of machine-gun fire from the Hezbollah, when the sector was overrun by the insurgents.

Lesson 7: I don't believe we need to compromise our principles or our convictions to be leaders and successful in business.

I wrote a book some time ago about the life and leadership secrets of H.J. Heinz. He was the "John Maxwell" of the 1860s and was demonstrating tremendous leadership principles far before leadership seminars were in vogue! He built an astounding worldwide successful company. It was not by accident. The actual title of the book is "It Was Never About the Ketchup!" [1] The title comes from a tremendous moment in the life of Mr. Heinz. After facing bankruptcy and the destruction of his company, many years later some financiers approached him to buy his successful operation. They offered him the argument that he had worked all his life and should "cash in" … and get a good, big price and enjoy the leisure to which he was entitled. It was an alluring proposal. He heard it all out and answered promptly:

> I don't care for your money, neither do I or my family wish to go out of business. We are not looking for ease or rest or freedom from responsibility. I love this business. Your talk of more money and less responsibility means nothing to me. To stop work is death … mentally and physically. This business is run not for my family or a few families, but for what we call the Heinz family … the people who make our goods

and sell them. The Heinz policy is to work for a better business rather than a bigger business; to make, if possible, a better product, and to make better people as we go along. We are working for success, and not for money. The money part will take care of itself."[2]

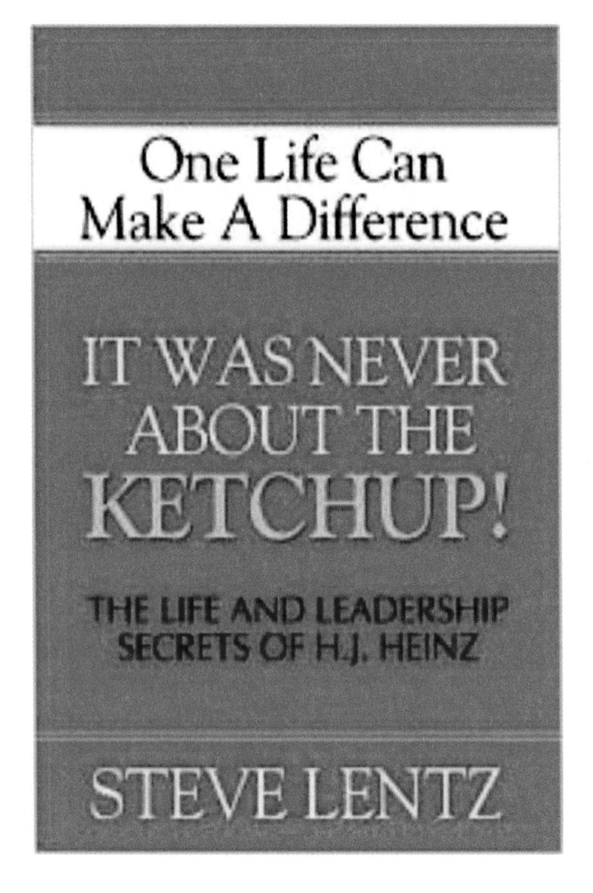

Can you imagine if this was the ethic and sentiment of corporate America today? "Working for success, and not for money … to make better people as we go along!" God's ways are not our ways. We don't have to look to conventional and fickle wisdom of this world for our direction. God's way is always the best! Jesus gave us the best path through when he warned us about wrong priorities:

> What good is it for someone to gain the whole world, yet forfeit their soul?[3]

At my previous law firm, Lentz Law Group, PLC, we had a set of Core Values that my staff was committed to. Frequently, we would read them as a group and then evaluate our performance based on these values. One of the Core Values of Lentz Law Group was "Honesty and Integrity." Our Core Values put it this way:

> At Lentz Law Group we are committed to providing each client with true and honest counsel and legal representation. At the same time, we will always be honest and

> straightforward with each other. We will strive to do what is right, in the right way and at the right time.

Our core scripture for this value was found in the book of Proverbs:

> The Lord abhors dishonest scales,
> but accurate weights are his delight.[4]

H. J. Heinz believed that truth was "not a pretty virtue to be admired. He considered truth to be as vital to a man as his vital organs."[5] An arresting story gives such a vivid picture of why truth was such a hallmark of this great business leader from the past.

H. J. Heinz believed that truth was "not a pretty virtue to be admired. He considered truth to be as vital to a man as his vital organs."

> One day he accosted a new employee at the weigher's platform weighing apples. The young man,

eager to impress his value on his employer said: "We are getting you a good weight today, Mr. Heinz." "Fine!" said Mr. Heinz. "What are you doing for me?" "Why, you know, a quick eye, a quick hand, and you can always slip over a few pounds extra!" Mr. Heinz nodded and after a moment asked him mildly to go with him to the office. When they arrived, he said: "Do you know what office this is? It's the cashier's office. You will be paid off, and you will leave this place at once." "But, Mr. Heinz!' cried the astonished young man, "I was saving you money!"

"You were robbing a man who was selling to me," said Mr. Heinz, "and you were robbing me of something more precious." As the young man exited, he added: "There is only one way to weigh or do anything else. Be as square to the other fellow as to yourself."

C. H. Spurgeon put it this way:

> It is clear … that our defense and our conquest must be obtained by sheer fighting. Many try compromise; but if you are a true Christian, you can never do this business well. The language of deceit fits not a holy tongue. The adversary is the father of lies, and those that are with him understand the art of equivocation; but saints abhor it.[6]

Lesson 8: TRUTH: It's a belt that holds everything else up in our life. We can't afford to compromise, or we might get caught "with our pants down"!

---

[1] *It Was Never About The Ketchup!* Copyright 2007. Steve Lentz

---

[2] Ibid., page 56-57.

[3] Mark 8:36 (NIV).

[4] Proverbs 11:1 (NIV).

[5] *It Was Never About the Ketchup*, page 13.

[6] A Sermon (No. 2201). Delivered on Lord's-Day Morning, April 19th, 1891, by C. H. SPURGEON, At the Metropolitan Tabernacle, Newington.

8

USE ALL THE EQUIPMENT! PART 2

"The Breastplate of Righteousness"
Protect Your Heart

I think the best analogy for today's sol-dier for the "breastplate of righteousness" is the flak jacket that is almost standard issue for any of our soldiers. The flak jacket protects primarily the heart. You can be wounded in a lot of places. You can even lose body parts in a battle and survive and lead an amazing, productive, and stellar life![1] But one thing is universally understood—we can't live without a heart!

The book of Proverbs has a lot to say about the importance of protecting our hearts.

> Keep vigilant watch over your
> heart;
> that's where life starts.[2]

> Keep thy heart with all diligence;
> for out of it are the issues of
> life.[3]

Almost everyone I saw in the war zone was wearing some kind of protection … especially over their heart. And for good reason. It reminded me so much of the admonishment in the Bible to protect our hearts.

Unfortunately, almost all of us have been wounded in some way by living our normal lives. Hurts, disappointments, and setbacks in relationships and in business have affected all of us if we are honest. For those of us in the faith community, the wounds from bad experiences from churches can be some of the most diabolical and difficult wounds to overcome and recover from. For any of us who have been wounded in any way, it is important to protect our hearts.

Some time ago, I read about a terrifying condition called Fibrodysplasia Ossifican Progressiva (FOP), sometimes called the "Stoneman Syndrome." It is a condition where the body overreacts to a bruise or a break. Instead of healing, the body begins to harden around the wounded area. [4] Individuals with FOB live their lives in fear of even minor injuries because of this disease. In its most extreme form, the entire body and organs turn to bone and the person becomes incapacitated and eventually dies. All from an overreaction to a hurt!

I think an important lesson that I learned from doing business in a war zone is to protect my heart. There are many reasons for all of us to harden our hearts. Disappointments in relationships and business. Disappointments and setbacks in our nuclear families and in our church experiences. Wounds from unfounded attacks. Misunderstandings. Failures in life. The list is unending. However, we need to continue to protect our hearts from getting hardened. Max Lucado once said:

> You live in a hard world, but you don't have to live with a hard heart.[5]

The Scriptures warn us that no good thing can come from allowing our hearts to be hardened in life.

> Blessed is the one who always
> trembles before God,
> but whoever hardens their heart
> falls into trouble.[6]

> With the Lord's authority I say this: Live no longer as the Gentiles do, for they are hopelessly confused. [18] Their minds are full of darkness; they wander far from the life God gives because they have closed their minds and hardened their hearts against him. [19] They have no sense of shame. They live for lustful pleasure and eagerly practice every kind of impurity.[7]

A hard heart ruins not only our own lives but also the lives of our family members and everyone we care about. Max Lucado noted the destructive character of a hard heart in our marriages:

> A hard heart ruins not only your life, but the lives of your family members. As an example, Jesus identified the hard heart as the wrecking ball of a marriage. When asked about divorce, Jesus said, "Moses permitted you to divorce your wives because our hearts were hard. But it was not this way from the beginning." (Matt. 19:8) When one or both people in a marriage stop trusting God to save it, they sign its death certificate. They reject the very one who can help them.[8]

I believe there are at least three essential elements that make up a good "flak jacket" to protect our hearts from becoming hardened in business, in church, and in life:

1. Keep a soft heart by remembering what God has done for you!

King David in the Bible understood how important it was to remember the goodness of God in our lives in order to keep a soft heart:

> God, don't just watch from the sidelines. Come on! Run to my side!
> My accusers—make them lose face. Those out to get me—make them look
> Like idiots, while I stretch out, reaching for you, and daily add praise to praise.
> I'll write the book on your righteousness, talk up your salvation the livelong day, never run out of good things to write or say.
> I come in the power of the Lord GOD, I post signs marking his right-of-way.[9]

King David's history is one of a leader hunted by enemies, betrayed by friends and family, and who faced many overwhelming challenges to his life and legacy.[10] And yet he understood the importance of keeping a soft heart by rehearsing the great things God had done for him. The book of Psalms is his tribute of "adding praise to praise" and his tribute of "never running out of good things to say" about the goodness of his God.

2. Keep a soft heart by watching your eyes!

> I will set no worthless thing before my eyes;
> I hate the work of those who fall away;
> It shall not fasten its grip on me.[11]

Remember Salam's eyes? He was watching for things that could hurt us. He was vigilant. He had "trained his eyes." Even after Salam and his family moved to the US and we would be out for a casual lunch in a restaurant, his eyes were always alert and watching.

Have we trained our eyes to spot the destructive things in our lives that can lead to bitterness and resentment? Things that can lead us to harden our hearts. Or are we still undaunted and looking for the good around us?

It always astonishes me when I read the Apostle Paul's letter to the Philippian church. He was in prison. They were free. And yet, he was encouraging them to "look on the good things"! Why? Because he was protecting his heart and wanted them to protect their hearts:

> Finally, brothers and sisters, whatever is true, whatever is noble, whatever is right, whatever is pure, whatever is lovely, whatever is admirable—if anything is excellent or praiseworthy—think about such things.[12]

3. Keep a soft heart by keeping communication open with God!

One of the best-known facts about the USA fighting force is its superior communications systems. Not only are we experts at keeping our lines of communication open, but we are experts at disabling the ability of our enemies to communicate with each other!

This same principle works in our everyday life. Our archenemy, the devil, is a master at trying to disrupt our communication lines to our God. If trouble or despair, hurt and disappointment, or bitterness and resentment can cause us to "shut down" our communication with God, then we have just exposed our hearts!

Prayer creates intimacy.
Intimacy keeps our hearts soft.

The Scriptures encourage us to maintain our vital personal relationship with God through prayer. Prayer creates intimacy, which keeps our hearts soft. I remember meeting with David Berkowitz at Sullivan State Prison in upstate New York. You might remember that Mr. Berkowitz was known as the Son of Sam.[13]

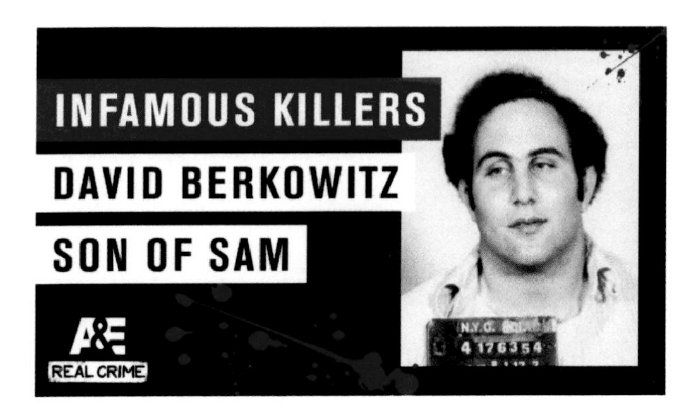

I was sent to interview him in the maximum-security prison. My friends had heard that he had given his life to Jesus and wanted me to interview him to evaluate the authenticity of his claim of becoming a Christian.

After doing thorough multiple searches throughout the prison, we set up a one-camera shoot in a room similar to a high school cafeteria. I sat my chair and the interview chair next to each other.

As Mr. Berkowitz was arriving, the guard asked, "Are you comfortable sitting that close to Mr. Berkowitz"?

I responded, "Are *you* comfortable with me sitting this close to Mr. Berkowitz?" I had never met him. He was a serial killer serving three consecutive life sentences. He had nothing to lose by assaulting me!

When he came in, he gave me a warm hug. We talked for about an hour as he testified about all that God had done in his life. He spoke about his gratitude that God would want anything to do with someone who had done such despicable acts and hurt so many people. His once heart of "stone" had been wonderfully softened by God's love, grace, and forgiveness.

I asked him the question that was perplexing me. I saw a man that would never see the outside of prison in his lifetime. I saw a man who had more peace and more meaning in his life than many of my very wealthy but troubled law clients. I had to ask, "David, how can someone like you, serving three life sentences, who will never get out of this place … how can you have hope"?

He answered with a gleam in his eye that I will never forget, "Steve, Jesus Christ *is* my hope." In spite of troubles. In spite of horrendous life experiences, David Berkowitz had found intimacy with God. Intimacy had given him a wonderful and contagious joy, peace, and a soft heart!

David Berkowitz as I met him after decades in prison—soft hearted and looking to his Savior for comfort and meaning in life

---

"Steve, Jesus Christ ***is*** *my hope."*

---

[1] Shout out to my good friend, Doug Greenlaw!

[2] Proverbs 4: 23 MSG.

[3] Proverbs 4: 23 KJV.

[4] **Fibrodysplasia ossificans progressiva** is a disorder in which muscle tissue and connective tissue such as tendons and ligaments are gradually replaced by bone (ossified), forming bone outside the skeleton (extra-skeletal or heterotopic bone) that constrains movement. It is a severe, disabling disorder with no cure or treatment and is the only known medical condition where one organ system changes into another. It slowly turns connective tissue such as tendons, muscles, and ligaments into bone....

[5] Max Lucado. "UpWords." From *3:16, The Numbers of Hope*
Copyright (W Publishing Group, 2007) Max Lucado.

[6] Proverbs 28:14 NIV.

[7] Ephesians 4: 17-19 NLT.

[8] Max Lucado. "UpWords." From *3:16, The Numbers of Hope*
Copyright (W Publishing Group, 2007) Max Lucado.

[9] Psalm 71:14-16 MSG.

[10] Did anyone mention killing the giant Goliath?

[11] Psalm 101:3 NASB.

---

[12] Philippians 4:8 NIV.

[13] **David Richard Berkowitz**, (born **Richard David Falco**, June 1, 1953), also known as the Son of Sam and the .44 Caliber Killer, is an American serial killer who pleaded guilty to eight separate shooting attacks that began in New York City during the summer of 1976.

9

USE ALL THE EQUIPMENT! PART 3

"Sword of the Spirit"

There is nothing worse than a dull and rusty sword! There is nothing passive about the urging in Ephesians for us to "Take the Sword"! I see this as a challenge. Spurgeon saw it as more than that. He called it "a word of thunder"!

> No man was ever holy by a happy chance. Infinite damage may be done by carelessness; but no man ever won life's battle by it. To let things go on as they please, is to let them bear us down to hell. We have no orders to be quiet and take

> matters easily. No; we are to pray always and watch constantly. The one note that rings out from the text is this: TAKE THE SWORD! TAKE THE SWORD! No longer is it, talk and debate! No longer is it parley and compromise! The word of thunder is *Take the sword*. The Captain's voice is clear as a trumpet-Take the sword! No Christian man here will have been obedient to our text unless with clear, sharp, and decisive firmness, courage, and resolve, he takes the sword. We must go to heaven sword in hand, all the way. "TAKE THE SWORD."[1]

The "full-armor of God" referenced in Ephesians chapter 6 has a lot of protective gear—the helmet, flak jacket, belt, shield, boots ... all well and good. But it makes no sense to go into a battle with no offensive weapons! That is where the "sword of the Spirit" comes in, which is a direct reference to the Holy Scriptures as a sword. I am informed by my faith, and I believe the Bible is absolutely the best handbook for life, for faith, and for business!

There is no doubt about the offensive "power" of the Holy Scriptures when we read about the temptation of Jesus in the wilderness. It was such a dramatic moment for our Savior, but also for the entire world. If Jesus had accepted the devil's offer to change his allegiance and leave his assignment, there would be no hope of salvation for the world! Jesus was being offered everything this world deems important—food, fame, and wealth. One hitch. It would have all been without going to the cross! Jesus could have called angels to help him; instead, he relied on the power of the sword of the Word of God. Jesus answered every temptation with a resounding, "It is written!"

> But Jesus said, *"It is written,* 'Man is not to live on bread only. Man is to live by every word that God speaks.'"
>
> Then the devil took Jesus up to Jerusalem, the holy city. He had Jesus stand on the highest part of the house of God. [6] The devil said to Him, "If You are the Son of God,

> throw Yourself down. It is written, 'He has told His angels to look after You. In their hands they will hold You up. Then Your foot will not hit against a stone.'"
>
> Jesus said to the devil, "*It is written* also, 'You must not tempt the Lord your God.'"
>
> Again the devil took Jesus to a very high mountain. He had Jesus look at all the nations of the world to see how great they were. [9] He said to Jesus, "I will give You all these nations if You will get down at my feet and worship me."
>
> Jesus said to the devil, "Get away, Satan. *It is written,* 'You must worship the Lord your God. You must obey Him only.'"[2]

When we step into the war zone of life, are we using *all* the equipment? In addition to resourcing ourselves with the power of the counsel from the Holy Scriptures, what kind of "ammunition" are we carrying? My guards in South Lebanon looked like they grabbed everything they could get their hands on—machine guns, side arms, bandoleros, knives, grenades, and even dogs! I think we need to load up on the ammunition available to us.

At least three vital pieces of ammunition should be part of our "standard issue" weapons:

1. Standard Issue Equipment: A Crack Legal Team

I know this can sound self-serving, but having the right legal team around you is essential to winning in battle. In my book: "The Business of Church," [3] I explain how important it is to select specialists who know who you are and what you are trying to accomplish.

I refer to my recent knee replacement surgery, due to an old basketball injury I sustained in the 70s playing in an adult league in college. The injury went virtually untreated until I finally became lame and could no longer function.

When it was time to get a knee replacement, I didn't go to my dentist! I went to a fabulous orthopedic surgeon. Both had medical degrees. Only one specialized in knee replacements! It was the best decision I ever made. His specialization in "zip surgery" minimized the damage done to my ligaments and tendons. My recovery time was insanely fast.

My point? Make sure you assemble a legal team that has a concentration in business. If you are a church, make sure the legal team understands both complex business and church law!

At Middle East Television, I actually had three different law firms under contract to help me navigate the complex legal layers of the Israel landscape. I had a contract lawyer (who I called my local "Columbo"). He was my bill collector. I had attorneys under contract in Jerusalem. They were orthodox Jews, and their job was to run interference for me when the ultra-conservative Jewish factions would harass us for being "outsiders" and threatening the Jewish-owned television empires of Channel 1 and Channel 2. I had a third law group that consisted of dashing Israeli fighter pilots. They were also leading the new, cutting-edge television, cable, and broadcast laws in Israel. Each had their expertise. Each protected me and enabled me to take ground for our superstation in Israel.

2. Standard-Issue Equipment: An Expert Accounting and Business Team

The financial complexities of the world we live in demand that we incorporate good accountants into our personal, church and business lives. My relationship with the accounting firm of KPMG saved me from embarrassment and possible business ruin while trying to develop business in Hong Kong and mainland China. As I was about to sign a development contract with my "friend," Danny Hoy, my accountants educated me that many of the Chinese companies had multiple sets of books!

Signing the business development deal between International Family Entertainment and Danny Hoy.

"Which set of books are they presenting to you for this deal?" they asked.

"What!" I said.

They compassionately explained, "In China, it is customary for a company to have at least three different sets of books—one for the owners, one for the auditors, and a third set for investors (suckers) like you."

Thank goodness I had a weapon on hand … my accounting team. We did the deal … but on the right set of books!

3. Standard Equipment: Business and Family Counselors

Throughout my marriage of nearly 50 years, throughout my spiritual life as an ordained minister, and throughout my varied business careers, I have never hesitated to seek counsel from marriage experts, spiritual leaders, and business experts.[4]

The Apostle Paul put it this way:

> Everyone who competes in the games goes into strict training. They do it to get a crown that will not last, but we do it to get a crown that will last forever. Therefore I do not run like someone running aimlessly; I do not fight like a boxer beating the air.[5]

I believe we desperately need counselors in our lives. Throughout our marriages, throughout our ministries, and throughout our business careers. We are foolish to think we can do this life on our own. Without good and trusted counselors, we end up "running aimlessly" and merely "boxing the air"!

---

[1] A Sermon (No. 2201). Delivered on Lord's-Day Morning, April 19th, 1891, by C. H. SPURGEON, At the Metropolitan Tabernacle, Newington.

[2] Matthew 4: 4-10 NLV, emphasis added.

[3] The Business of Church. ©2019 Stephen D. Lentz, Esq.

[4] Shout out to my good friend for over 40 years, Dr. Eric Scalise, president of LIV Enterprises & Consulting, LLC. He currently serves as Senior Vice President and Chief Strategy Officer with *Hope for the Heart*, an international Christian counseling ministry offering biblical hope and practical help. Eric has been part of the fabric of the Lentz family for over 40 years. His wisdom and counsel have been invaluable to our family.

[5] I Corinthians 9:25-26 NIV.

10

HAVING DONE ALL ... STAND!

I want to finish this book with probably the most important lesson in the Ephesians 6 list of armor. It isn't actually a piece of armor at all. It is an attitude!

> Therefore put on the full armor of God, so that when the day of evil comes, you may be able to stand your ground, and after you have done everything, to stand.[1]

I have met so many talented and gifted men and women who give up too soon! Couples who give up on their marriages. Ministers who give up on their vision for the church. Businessmen and women who walk away from their dreams too soon! The passage ends with a secret to power ... STAND! Just refuse to leave the field. Good things can happen when we refuse to give up. There are so many examples of people we look up to in history who just refused to quit!

Many businesses and sociologists refer to a phenomenon called the "Failure Trap." Much public attention is paid to people who are highly successful, says Siimon Reynolds, a high-performance business coach and author of *Why People Fail.*

"We ought to start championing people who fail intelligently ... who fail forward."
–Siimon Reynolds

People who get to the top typically have had more failures than successes. "We ought to start championing people who fail intelligently ... who fail forward."

Failure can either break us or make us. Those broken by failure can be haunted by unpleasant memories. Failure memories can be like shadows that lurk in front, behind, beside, beneath, and above. They can be like a prison that traps the mind, preventing it from entertaining the possibilities of freedom and success. People in this cycle can become convinced that they cannot do it; therefore, they will not try.

Overcoming failure takes more than "mental toughness" and "fervent initiative." I believe overcoming failure takes perspective!

Overcoming failure takes PERSPECTIVE!

Mistakes are inevitable in every profession. I have failed multiple times in my ministry and business career. In my first experience as an associate pastor in Williamsburg, Virginia, I had a falling out with a controlling pastor. I was excommunicated from the congregation I loved when I actually challenged my motives and the leadership's motives for serving. I left the people I loved. I was devastated. Years later, my faith and love for the local church was restored by meeting wonderful servants of God and by being introduced to the exciting world of today's emerging churches.[2]

I was fired from my first law job! After being excommunicated from my church, I was hired as a beginning associate at a law firm in Chesapeake, Virginia. I was actually an emotional wreck. I felt I had landed on Mars. I thought I would pastor for the rest of my life at the lovely church in Williamsburg. Because I had to start over, my salary was very small. I had a family of six, so I worked many side jobs to supplement my income. I pressure washed houses and worked as a janitor at a Christian School to pay for tuition for my children. I also worked as a night auditor at a hotel. And, finally, I worked in a juvenile detention home on the locked ward on the graveyard shift. Honestly, I thought my life had ended and that God had banished me to hell! I was eventually fired because I couldn't keep up with my work.[3] Fast forward 30 years later and I have the privilege of stewarding a national and international legal practice with clients in all 50 states and every province of Canada. God had a plan. I just needed perspective!

If you feel that you have taken some hits by being on the battlefield of life, be comforted. You are in good company. Someone once said, *"True failure only happens when one gives up!"* Consider this celebrity list of potential failures who did not give up:

Remember, that failures are only permanent if we stop trying.

- **Marilyn Monroe**, in 1947, after one year under contract, was dropped by 20th Century-Fox because Darryl Zanuck thought she was unattractive.
- **John Grisham's** first novel, *A Time to Kill*, was rejected by 16 agents and a dozen publishing houses.
- **Walt Disney's** first cartoon production company went bankrupt.
- **Barbra Streisand** made her stage debut at age 19 in a show that opened and closed in a single night.
- **Babe Ruth** spent his childhood years in an orphanage and, as a baseball player, struck out 1,330 times . . . on his way to the Hall of Fame.

- **Elvis Presley** was banished from the Grand Ole Opry after one performance and was told, "You ain't goin' nowhere, son."
- **Oprah Winfrey** was fired from her television reporter's job and advised, "You're not fit for TV."
- **Albert Einstein** failed the entrance exams to the Swiss Polytechnic Institute.
- **Muhammad Ali** graduated 376th from a high school class of 391 students.
- **Julia Roberts** auditioned for All My Children but didn't get the part.
- **J. K. Rowling** (author of the Harry Potter novels) who was so impoverished that she lived on welfare in an apartment infested with mice.
- **Sharon Stone** could not get a date to her own high school prom dance.

- **John Wayne** was rejected by the United States Naval Academy.
- **Steve Jobs** (founder of Apple Computer) dropped out of Reed College in his freshman year.

Probably the most poignant list of failures is represented by the career of President Abraham Lincoln.

History has been kind to President Lincoln. He has been painted as probably the greatest president of the United States of America. It is a good thing that history also recorded his failures. It reflected his frail humanity but also showed his attitude of never giving up.

Consider his ups and downs in his political life:

1831 – Failed in business
1832 – Defeated for legislature
1833 – Again failed in business
1834 – Elected to legislature
1835 – Sweetheart died
1836 – Had a nervous breakdown

1838 – Defeated for speaker
1840 – Defeated for elector
1843 – Defeated for Congress
1846 – Elected for Congress
1848 – Defeated for Congress
1855 – Defeated for Senate
1856 – Defeated for vice-president
1858 – Defeated for Senate
1860 – ELECTED PRESIDENT

He was defeated more times than he won, but that did not mean he was a failure. Remember that failures are only permanent if we stop trying. I believe the only real failure is the failure not to move on.

My great concern is not whether you have failed, but whether you are content with your failure. – Abraham Lincoln

---

I have a good friend. His name is Jake Steinfeld. You may recognize him through his brand "Body by Jake." I had the privilege of working as the president and CEO of a television network that Jake founded: "FitTV." It was Jake's idea. It was Jake's concept. He understood how to market and promote and program this sweet little network. And it made good money! Eventually, the network was purchased by Discovery Network.[4] Here is where the story gets interesting.

At the NASCAR sponsorship with Jake and NASCAR legend Mark Martin

Jake's motto throughout his career has been: "Don't Quit."

He proved it during the FitTV journey. When we started the network, Jake requested a clause in his ownership contract ensuring that he would always have the "first right of refusal" if the channel was ever sold. As the network changed hands multiple times, the new owners tried to marginalize him and push him out of the channel. Key executives insulted him and disrespected him. At one point he was told in a condescending way, "You are like Jack Nicklaus is to the Golf Channel—you don't have to be on the air anymore!" (They did not mean it as a compliment!) But Jake would not quit! Having done everything he knew to do to make the channel a success, he stood!

One day, while I was working at my desk in Virginia Beach, Jake called me. "Skipper," (Jake gives everyone he knows a nickname ... don't ask!) "I just want to thank you for working with me to get that first-right-of-refusal clause in my contract."

He explained that FitTV had just changed hands again, (he actually learned about it when he was reading the *Wall Street Journal*), but he was not given the chance to buy it. "I had my lawyers call the former owners. We had a meeting in my office. My attorney told them they might be interested to know they just sold something they didn't have a right to sell"! The network attorneys read the contract, looked up, and basically asked me to name my price!" On the phone call, Jake went on to thank me for the multi-million-dollar check that he had in his hand! Jake was sure glad he didn't quit!

Having done all ... STAND.
Don't Quit! Your best days are ahead of you!

---

[1] Ephesians 6: 13 NIV.

[2] My son, Carl Lentz, now pastors Hillsong NYC and is having an impact on thousands of people weekly. I am so glad I did not give up on the local church!

[3] I was actually exhausted, working some nights all night and returning to my "day job" at the law firm with little or no sleep. I was working five other jobs on the side to keep my family above water. I never disclosed the outside jobs to the partners.

[4] **FitTV** was an American pay television channel, owned by Discovery Communications. The channel focused on fitness and exercise-related programming. FitTV offered programming with such fitness celebrities as Cathe Friedrich, Sharon Mann, Gilad

Janklowicz, Marilu Henner, Tamilee Webb, and others. On February 1, 2011, it merged with Discovery Health Channel to become Discovery Fit & Health, now known as Discovery Life.

ABOUT THE AUTHOR

Stephen D. Lentz, Esq.
381 Edwin Drive
Virginia Beach, VA
slentz@ectlawyers.com
www.eastcoasttriallawyers.com
www.stephendlentz.com

Stephen D. Lentz is Senior Counsel with East Coast Trial Lawyers, PLC in Virginia Beach, Virginia and manages the non-profit and complex business law division of the firm. He is licensed to practice law in Virginia and Tennessee.

Prior to joining East Coast Trial Lawyers, Mr. Lentz guided his former firm, Lentz Law Group, which he founded, to become a boutique business and estate-planning practice, serving clients in the areas of corporate formation, complex business transactions, entertainment law, intellectual property, non-profit law, foundation and church/ministry representation, simple and complex estate planning, and elder law. He has counseled corporations and non-profit organizations in both the United States and around the world.

Mr. Lentz is recognized as one of the top 5 "Church Law Authorities" in the U.S., representing denominations and churches in all 50 states and every province in Canada. He has also been recognized as one of the "Top Lawyers of Coastal Virginia" in 2018–2019 and 2020 in the area of non-profit law by *Coastal Virginia Magazine*.

In addition to his legal practice, Mr. Lentz serves as an adjunct professor at Regent

University School of Law, where he has taught Wills, Trusts & Estates, Law Practice Management, International Business Transactions, and Entertainment Law. He also served as adjunct faculty of Regent University's Graduate School of Communications, where he taught Media Law, Policy and Ethics.

Prior to establishing the Lentz Law Group in Tidewater, Virginia, Mr. Lentz spent 15 years in the television industry. From 1997–2000, he was the President of Middle East Television. He was responsible for crafting the legal strategy to change the commercial broadcast laws in Israel to permit non-Israeli television entities from running advertising targeted at Israel. Middle East Television became the largest super-station in the Middle East, reaching a potential audience of over 100 million viewers in 17 Arab countries and all of Israel. Mr. Lentz functioned as in-house counsel and appeared either in person or by counsel before the Israeli Supreme Court six times in the 14 months prior to 1999.

From 1993 to 1997, Mr. Lentz was the president and CEO of FitTV and was instrumental in building the company into an attractive national niche cable network. As in-house counsel, he was responsible for both employment and television broadcast law compliance as well as entertainment contracts. During this time, he regularly dealt with issues related to interstate commercial law and emerging cyber-law issues. He helped craft the strategy to sell the company to Fox Sports in 1997.

From 1985–1993, Mr. Lentz was the senior vice president of Worldwide Sales for International Family Entertainment, where he managed advertising sales offices in New York, Chicago, Detroit, Los Angeles, London, and Hong Kong. He was responsible for generating over $100 million per year in revenue to substantiate the valuation of the company in its sale to Rupert Murdock in 1997. He was part of the strategic management team that led to International Family Entertainment's successful IPO and later sale to Rupert Murdoch for $1.9 billion.

Mr. Lentz received his Bachelor of Arts from Bowling Green State University in Bowling Green, Ohio in 1971, and his Juris Doctor from the Marshal-Wythe School of Law, College of William and Mary, in Williamsburg, Virginia in 1976.

Mr. Lentz has authored two business leadership books:

- *It Was Never About the Ketchup: The Life and Leadership Secrets of H.J. Heinz*
- *The Business of Church: The Essential Business Handbook For Pastors*

He has been married to his high-school sweetheart, Catherine Lentz, for 47 years and has four married adult children and seven grandchildren. He has lived in Virginia Beach, Virginia for the past 29 years.